William Van Horne

Stephen Mayles

Fitzhenry & Whiteside Limited

Contents

The Author

Stephen Mayles lives in Toronto, and is a former high school history teacher. He has written an earlier book on the Canadian Pacific Railway, and is currently working on a new biography for the Canadians *series.*

© *1976 Fitzhenry & Whiteside Limited*
    150 Lesmill Road
    Don Mills, Ontario, M3B 2T5

Printed and bound in Canada

ISBN-0-88902-216-X

Early Days Chapter 1

One of William Van Horne's lasting childhood memories was of chopping wood. He hated it. After school, there were always lots of chores to be done, and William was eager to help his widowed mother keep up their cottage. There was wood to be chopped, grass to be cut, floors to be swept, garbage to be burned. The list was a long one, and William cheerfully performed each task. He liked the work. Except for the wood chopping. He wasn't quite sure just what it was about chopping wood that made him hate it so. Perhaps it was the sheer monotony of the work. He only knew that he had to force himself to pick up the axe every time, and force his feet to move in the direction of the wood pile. It was awful. But the wood was there. It had to be chopped. So William did it. Later in his life he said, "Chopping wood was the only real work I ever did."

William Cornelius Van Horne was born on February 3, 1843 in Chelsea, Illinois. He was the first of five children born to Cornelius Van Horne and his second wife, Mary Miner Richards.

William's father was a lawyer who had moved from New York to Illinois in 1832. After his first wife and children died, Cornelius Van Horne purchased a 360-acre farm near Chelsea, where he remarried. The farm had a stable, a saw mill, and a variety of other out-buildings. This was William's birthplace.

William's early years were spent in a politically oriented household. His father was the first Justice of the Peace for the Chelsea district, and would ride to the capital from time to time on legal business. There he often met and visited with his fellow lawyers, including Abraham Lincoln and Stephen Douglas. In 1851, William's father moved his family to Joliet, a growing community of some 2000 people. He became Joliet's first mayor in 1852.

William's schooling was relatively brief, and ended when he was fourteen. He was a lazy student, but he had

Cornelius Van Horne

a lively intelligence and an active imagination which served him well. He played games only rarely, but he was an eager fighter, and accepted challenges from anyone. William's chief amusements were reading, and drawing caricatures of his classmates, teachers and faces from magazines. His favourite victims were the American authors whose pictures were featured in *Harper's* Magazine. His alterations to these people's faces were so skillfully done that his mother once remarked to her friends that she couldn't understand why the editors of *Harper's* would allow such disparaging portraits to appear in their magazine. One day as William was finishing a particularly ludicrous portrait of the principal, he was caught. The principal was not amused. He marched William off to his office and gave the boy a severe caning. William was not amused either. He never went back.

Much of William's knowledge was self-taught. As a young child, his first great possession was a slate pebble which he used to draw pictures on his school slate. Eventually the pebble wore down to nothing. William was forced to find another toy. One day, while walking down the main street of town, he discovered a perfect trilobite embedded in a slab of stone. Returning later that night with a hammer and lantern, he pried the figure loose, and promptly named it "worm-in-the-rock." William was immensely proud of his new find. He carried it about with him constantly, showing it to all his friends. The rock became a treasured possession, not only in William's mind, but also in the minds of his friends, because it was the only figure of its kind to be found.

A few years later, William discovered his "worm-in-the-rock" again in an illustrated history of a New York county. This discovery signalled the beginning of his passion for geology, and he decided to learn all he could about the subject. When he found that one of his friends, Augustus Howk, actually owned a book on geology, William knew he had picked the right hobby. He borrowed the book, and laboriously copied it page by page — text, illustrations, and index (262 pages in all). The task took him five weeks, but it was worth every minute. Later in his life, William described his experience in these words:

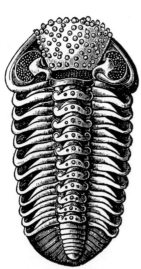

Trilobites were prehistoric sea animals, probably scavengers which fed on material found on the ocean floor. Trilobite fossils are important clues to early Paleozoic development. Can you find examples of trilobites that differ from the one above?

The copying of that book did great things for me. It taught me
how much could be accomplished by application; it improved my
handwriting; it taught me the construction of English sentences;
and it helped my drawing materially. And I never had to refer to
the book again.

William was also interested in art, and he became an
entrepreneur at an early age — trading his skills as an
artist for money. Once he exhibited an impressive pano-
rama of the Crystal Palace in London, England (which he
copied from a picture in *Harper's* Magazine). This pano-
rama, mounted on rollers and ingeniously fitted with a
crank, was estimated to be "several score of feet in
length." Working together with two partners, William
held his extravanganza in a tent with an admission fee of
a penny. He raised the price as soon as he noticed the
show's popularity.

Suddenly in 1854, tragedy struck the family. Cornelius Van Horne died of cholera, leaving a pile of debts
and very little money. Times were hard, and William's
father had been a generous man, often providing his
services free of charge. His son later reflected on this
practice in a letter to his own grandson in 1914:

I can remember him refusing payment for services not once, but
many times, when I felt sure that he had not a penny in his pocket.
I could not understand it then and I am not quite sure that I do
now, but this occurred in a newly settled country where all were
poor alike.
  My mother was a noble woman, courageous and resourceful,
and she managed to find bread . . . and to keep us in school until
I was able to earn something — which I had to set about at
fourteen.

The Van Horne family's financial picture changed
drastically. They were forced to leave their comfortable
surroundings and move to a small cottage in Joliet. One
of William's brothers went to live with a family friend.

In order to help his mother feed the family, William
took a job carrying telegraph messages. When not out
on the streets delivering telegrams, he would sit around
the office listening to the sounds of the instruments and
watching the slow unwinding of the tape that spelled out
the messages in dots and dashes. William was fascinated,
and he learned much by quietly watching and paying
attention to the office routines. Telegraphy was not all he

learned at this first job, however. His fellow workers plied him with bits of hard-headed wisdom, numerous tall tales and yarns, and even introduced him to the game of poker, which William later described as "not a game but an education."

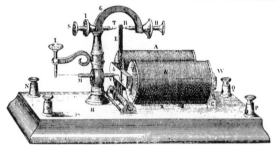

The early telegraph receiver produced messages through the use of a stylus which marked the appropriate dots and dashes on paper strips. The telegraph relay was another important part of the system. Can you find out how it worked?

The Youthful Railroader

Chapter 2

In 1856 Abraham Lincoln came to Joliet on an early leg of the political campaign which was to lead him to the White House. By this time William had graduated from messenger boy to telegrapher, and had become expert enough in his job to assist in sending out reports of Lincoln's reception and speech. In the spring of 1857 he was hired by the Illinois Central Railway Company as a telegrapher and sent to Chicago.

William was an ambitious worker, and exhibited the same desire for leadership at business that he had at school. He realized that a young boy working in an adult world had only the judicious use of his wits with which to get ahead. And William was determined to get ahead.

Not that he was an overly serious worker. Indeed, he often enjoyed playing practical jokes on his associates. One day he ran a ground wire from the boss's office to a steel plate in the railway yards (which could be seen from his window). The wire was charged with electricity, and any man who stepped on the steel plate received a shock. William was highly entertained by the spectacle. Then William's boss stepped on the plate. Unlike William's other victims, the boss knew something about electricity.

Clark Street, Chicago, 1857. Note the different levels of the sidewalk. Why might this have been done?

He looked down, saw the wire, and followed it to its source in his office. Hot with anger, the boss collared William and asked him to explain. William suggested that it was only a practical joke. The boss was not amused, and with a few choice words, kicked William out of the office, telling him not to return. Thus ended Van Horne's association with the Illinois Central Railway. He went back to Joliet.

Shortly thereafter, William was hired by the Michigan Central Railway as a freight-checker and messenger for a section of track 40 miles long. His wage was fifteen dollars a month, and he was able to stay in Joliet — now a thriving little city with considerable freight business. The job brought him into contact with the businessmen of the community who were impressed with his intelligence and industriousness.

William was ambitious, and before long he approached his new superintendent with an idea for an independent telegraph line, which he volunteered to run. The line was installed. In 1858, fifteen-year-old Van Horne sent the report over the wire of the famous debates between Lincoln and Douglas on the slavery question.

Lincoln-Douglas debate in Illinois.

With practice, William became more and more expert at the telegraph. His reputation spread, yet this was not enough for the enterprising young businessman. He began to study the jobs of his fellow office workers — cashier, timekeeper, accountant, and all the others. Soon William had a fairly accurate idea of what every person in his office did. He would even slip into the drawing offices at lunch and after hours to copy from the draftsmen's books — a practice which helped him acquire a knowledge of art principles. One of the draftsmen was astonished by William's drawings and often used his talent for fine lettering. Van Horne also possessed a remarkable memory. He would memorize the numbers on the cars of a long freight train as it passed by his window. He delighted in challenging his associates to memory contests, and he usually won.

After a visit to the yards by the General Superintendent, William's goal became more concrete:

I found myself wondering if even I might not somehow become a General Superintendent and travel in a private car. The glories of it, the pride of it, the salary pertaining to it, and all that moved me deeply, and I made up my mind then and there that I would reach it. And I did ten years later, at the age of twenty-eight.

The goal I had promised myself was never out of my mind, and I avoided every path, however attractive, that did not lead in its direction. I imagined that a General Superintendent must know everything about a railway — every detail in every department — and my working hours were no longer governed by the clock. I took no holidays, but gladly took up the work of others who did, and I worked nights and Sundays to keep it all going without neglecting my own tasks. So I became acquainted with all sorts of things I could not otherwise have known. I found time to haunt the repairshops and to become familiar with materials and tools and machinery and methods — familiar with locomotives and cars and all pertaining to them — and to learn line repairs from the roadmaster and the section-hands — something of bridges from the engineer, and so on. And there were opportunities to drive locomotives and conduct trains. And not any of this could be called work for it was a constant source of pleasure.

Despite Van Horne's growing interest and involvement in the business world, he remained very close to his family. He loved to bring his mother presents — a new hat, dress, material, even new furniture. The type and cost of each gift varied with the size of the boy's salary, but William was making an early start on the cultivation of the good taste he would exhibit later in his life.

One day, shortly after the outbreak of the Civil War, William slipped quietly away from the office and enlisted in the Federal Army. He supported the Union and wanted to fight in its behalf. But who would look after his widowed mother? Who would handle his telegraphy duties? When William's superintendent found out about his enlistment, he immediately arranged for the boy's release. The Civil War caused many cutbacks in the staff at the telegraph office but William was kept on. He soon proved to be his superintendent's right hand man.

William retained his love of practical jokes, even though his work load was now a large one. One day, while he was in charge of the office, some gravel cars escaped from the pit-master, a man named Glassford. They raced crazily through the yard, ultimately smashing into the repair shops, where a man named Williamson was foreman. Van Horne sent the following report to his boss: "George B. Glassford stormed Fort Williamson this morning with a battery of four cars of gravel and completely demolished the fort." Another time, word came out from Van Horne's office of a great Union victory.

The War for the Union, 1862 — A bayonet charge.

The report detailed splendid and exciting events. The people of Joliet were delighted. They paraded, sang, and raised the Union flag. When the Chicago newspapers arrived, however, there was no mention of any Union victory. They did not even report a battle! William had made up the story. Angry townspeople rushed to the telegraph office to catch the practical joker. William was not to be found. He was sitting at home quietly chuckling over the whole incident.

In 1862, Van Horne was offered the position of operator and ticket-agent for the Chicago and Alton Railway at Joliet. The job brought him a substantial increase in salary, but more importantly, it also brought him directly under the observation of top officials. The work was challenging. It was his first experience in managing people, and William quickly began to show his resourcefulness. He set up a crude but effective cold storage area for preserving farmers' butter. The idea worked so well that the railway constructed similar areas at the other stations along its route.

William's work days were long and hard, and he spent his nights reading and studying. It was difficult to wake up early in the morning. A common sight for the townspeople of Joliet was young Van Horne racing to the station to catch the first train. William's mother worried

Chicago and Alton Depot, Joliet, Illinois.

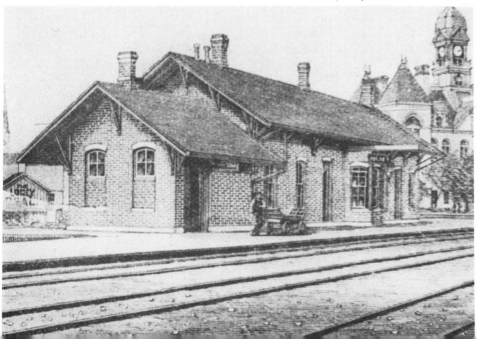

about him and usually slipped a couple of breakfast buns into his hand as he dashed out the door. "You'll never amount to anything if you don't learn to go to bed and rise early," she warned him.

One Sunday in 1866, Willaim surprised his family by announcing his engagement to Lucy Adaline Hurd, the daughter of a Joliet civil engineer. Lucy was a beautiful girl whom one admirer described as "tall, slender, and dignified, with softly waving black hair, hazel eyes, and an apple blossom complexion." The couple had met two years earlier when Lucy was returning from a trip to Chicago. After an awkward introduction — William was so nervous he set his jacket afire by stuffing a lighted pipe into his pocket — the two saw much of each other, but it was not until 1867 that they were able to marry.

The Van Horne household was a busy one for, soon after the marriage, William's mother, his sister Mary, and Lucy's mother, all came to live with them. All four women idolized Van Horne, so the unusual arrangement was a harmonious success. In 1868, Lucy gave birth to a daughter, Adaline, just in time for the family's move to Alton, where William was promoted to Superintendent of Telegraphs for the Chicago and Alton. William, the second child, was born in October 1871, the day before the great Chicago fire, but died at the age of five. A second son, Richard Benedict, was born some years later in 1877.

Lucy Adaline Van Horne in middle age.

In 1872, at the age of 29, Van Horne was appointed General Manager of the St. Louis, Kansas City and Northern Railway (a subsidiary of the Chicago and Alton). He and his family moved to St. Louis. Shortly after the move, Lucy caught smallpox. Although the normal procedure in such cases was to send the invalid to the pesthouse, William chose to nurse his wife himself. During the day, he isolated himself in the attic study with Lucy. At night, he changed his clothes, disinfected himself, and went to work. The nursing was successful. Lucy made a good recovery, with few disfiguring marks, and the disease was not given to any other member of the family.

Within two years, Van Horne succeeded in putting the St. Louis, Kansas City and Northern back on its feet, winning great acclaim for himself in the process. In 1874, however, disagreement arose among the line's directors, and two of them sold out their shares. These two men then persuaded Van Horne to become the President and General Manager of the Southern Minnesota Railway — 167 miles long, and bankrupt.

It was a particularly challenging position. Van Horne set to work. He sought to increase revenues by attracting wheat shippers. His efforts resulted in a significant increase within six months. He ordered free lunches for all the railway workers, believing that happy crews increase work output. He subsidized farmers who settled along the Southern Minnesota tracks, and cut operating expenses from 72% of earnings to 56%. When the farmers were struck by a grasshopper plague, Van Horne concocted a horse-drawn sheet iron pan which, when smeared with tar and pulled through the fields, attracted the insects to their death. "Praying won't move one grasshopper," he admonished a group of farmers. "What you've got to do is take your coats off and hustle!" His efforts resulted in the salvation of most of the farmers' crops — which were then shipped to buyers by the Southern Minnesota.

Moving from administration to construction, Van Horne began building onto the Southern Minnesota tracks, to make the line complete. This phase of his work brought him into contact with politicians, a breed of men he found distasteful. Before completing the Southern Minnesota line, Van Horne was asked by the Chicago, Milwaukee and St. Paul Railway to act as its general superintendent. He accept the job, but stipulated in his acceptance, that he be allowed to keep the presidency of the Southern Minnesota until the line was completed. His new position brought Van Horne into an ever increasing circle of influential railroad men, James Jerome Hill among them. A Canadian stock promoter from Galt, Ontario, Hill was also co-partner (with Donald Smith and George Stephen) of the St. Paul, Minneapolis and Manitoba Railway, which extended into Canada north to Winnipeg. Hill was an important man to know, and it was from him that Van Horne first learned the ambitious plans for a Canadian transcontinental railway.

James Jerome Hill, founder of the Great Northern Railroad, was one of the most successful railroad kings in United States' history. His personal fortune was an estimated sixty million dollars.

Chapter 3 The Coming of the Canadian Pacific

When the Dominion of Canada was formed in 1867, it included only the provinces of Ontario, Quebec, New Brunswick and Nova Scotia. The area west of Lake Huron extending to the Pacific Coast was wilderness. The majority of settlers in this region were employees of the Hudson's Bay Company and their families. Mountain ranges effectively isolated the westerners from settlers on the prairies and in eastern Canada. The small but thriving community on Vancouver Island had easy access to American ports but no ready access to the areas east of the Rocky Mountains. It was not until 1858, however, when gold was discovered in the Cariboo district, that the difficulties of access became a matter of national concern. Miners from Quebec and Ontario who wanted to reach the goldfields in British Columbia were forced to make a long trip by railway and stagecoach across the western United States, or by steamship from the east coast of the United States to the Pacific Coast, crossing the Isthmus of Panama by railway.

In 1871 the Articles of Confederation, which added British Columbia to the Canadian nation, stipulated that a railway should link this new western province with its eastern counterparts within ten years. Growing feelings of national unity focussed public attention on the need for a transcontinental railway. The first Riel rebellion in 1870 illustrated even more graphically the necessity for such a link when Canadian troops took 90 days to reach Fort Gary from Toronto over the best possible route. Canadian politicians eyed the completion of the first American transcontinental railway in 1869 with envy and misgiving. On March 31, 1870, the Toronto *Globe* echoed the feelings of many Canadians

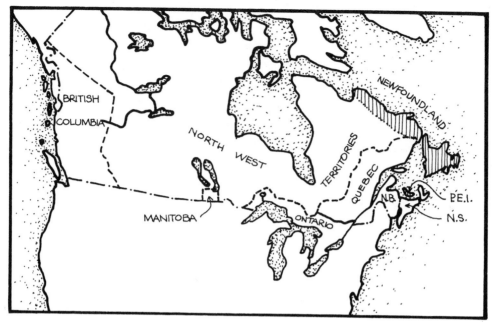

Canada in 1871

when it printed that, "With the construction of the railway, the country will be populated by Canadians; without
it, by Americans." Clearly the time had come, econom-
ically, politically, and strategically, for Canada to begin
work on her own nationwide railsystem.

Negotiations for the building of the railway began,
but there were many problems and obstacles to be over-
come. The population of Canada was four million people,
and the young nation was not wealthy. The railway project would require estimated funding of $100,000,000, and
the work of many thousand labourers. Where and how
would the money be raised? Was it possible to build a
railway through the Rocky Mountains? How would a
railway affect the native peoples? Would such a venture
ever prove financially successful, for there were very few
people living on the prairies?

The Canadian government, under the leadership of
Sir John A. Macdonald as Prime Minister, had originally
hoped to control the work, but have the railway built and
operated by private business. The government would
grant land and money to the project — but no additional
levies would be laid on the Canadian taxpayer. Macdonald's government was already involved in railroad

Sir John A. Macdonald

construction at this time as it had committed itself to the completion of the Intercolonial Railway — connecting Ontario and Quebec to New Brunswick and Nova Scotia. This project was a costly one, and would take another five years to complete. The additional burden of a transcontinental railway would prove to be unwieldy for the government, and Macdonald hunted for a private group of entrepreneurs to undertake the task.

The government assumed the job of surveying proposed routes for the transcontinental line, and in 1872, it granted charters to two private companies who would undertake the actual construction. These early contracts proved unsuccessful, however, due to political and business complications, scandal, and economic depression. Macdonald himself fell from power when it was revealed that the principal figure in one of the railway companies had contributed substantially to his Conservative Party's funds. In 1873 Alexander Mackenzie and the Liberals assumed leadership of the government. Mackenzie was not an enthusiastic supporter of a trans-Canada railway, especially as the Canadian economic situation was unstable. Nevertheless, he sought to effect a compromise by proposing an alternate rail-water route to be constructed from Ottawa, northwest to Gergian Bay, then west to the Lake of the Woods. The Mackenzie government would also undertake or support the construction of a railroad from Winnipeg to the Southern Manitoba border — for a link-up with a U.S. line. These piecemeal policies were initiated, but as John A. Macdonald returned to power in 1878, they were merely incorporated into the larger, broader scheme of a fully Canadian transcontinental railroad.

In the spring of 1880, Macdonald met with a group of Montreal capitalists who agreed to undertake the full construction of the transcontinental railway. The Canadian Pacific Railway Company "CPR Syndicate" was formed in February 1881 by Donald Smith, George Stephen, Duncan McIntyre and James Hill. The company was granted a charter, and George Stephen became the first president. The CPR began operations in May 1881 by assuming control of the government-built lines in Manitoba and undertaking further construction. Hill, Stephen, McIntyre and Smith were basically financiers and political wheeler-dealers. They had the experience and drive necessary to get the Canadian Pacific off the ground initially, but it soon became apparent that they needed someone to assume the mammoth task of overseeing the actual building process. They needed a general manager. Hill insisted that Van Horne be hired. "He's the only man for the construction job — he's the best equipped mentally and every other way. But he will take all the authority he gets and more, so define how much you want him to have."

Donald Smith

Van Horne was interviewed by the other members of the "Syndicate" who were impressed. They agreed with Hill's assessment, and offered Van Horne the job of General Manager of the Canadian Pacific Railway, at a salary of $15,000 a year — the highest ever paid to a western railroading man. The offer was accepted. Van Horne began to marshall his energies for his new position, which would begin officially on January 1, 1882.

Chapter 4 **Laying the First Tracks**

William Van Horne at 39

Van Horne was thirty-eight years old when he stepped off the train in Winnipeg on December 31, 1881 to assume his new duties as General Manager of the Canadian Pacific Railway. He was a large man, inclined to corpulence, with a bushy beard and dark, piercing eyes. He had a large, bull-like head with a high forehead, and a rather large nose. There was usually a cigar in his mouth. He looked very much like what he was — the successful businessman, accustomed to giving orders and to having them obeyed. His welcome in Winnipeg was not auspicious. The temperature was 42 below zero and the land was deep in the grip of winter. The town was snow-covered, and a frigid, biting Arctic wind raged through the streets.

Van Horne established his offices on the second floor of the Bank of Montreal building and immediately set to work. His task: to lay over 2900 miles of track across largely unexplored terrain as quickly as possible. From the outset there were problems. The English engineers resented this new big, bluff outsider with a fat cigar in his mouth. His coarse language, laced liberally with four-letter words, his bluntness and lack of tact, his arrogant handling of subordinates, his emphasis on total honesty and commitment to the company, his unflagging energy, and his ruthless efficiency were all characteristics the engineers found difficult to accept. One senior engineer, J. H. E. Secretan, echoed the feelings of many others when he wrote:

Van Horne was a great man with a gigantic intellect, a generous soul and an enormous capacity for food and work . . . but we did not like him when he first came up to Winnipeg as General Boss of Everybody and Everything. His ways were not our ways, and he did not hesitate to let us know what he thought of us . . . he told me that if he could only teach the section men to run a transit, he wouldn't have a single damn engineer about the place.

Van Horne's assumption of power was immediate, and it was not long after this first day on the job that he announced the CPR would lay 500 miles of track during the 1882 season. This statement was greeted as no more than an idle boast at first, especially when people realized that the Canadian Government had spent millions of dollars over a ten-year period to produce 300 miles of track. In 1881 the CPR itself had only managed to lay 100 miles of track to Flat Creek (now Oak Lake), 161 miles west of Winnipeg. The 500 miles, if finished, would bring the track to the South Saskatchewan River at Medicine Hat, 661 miles west of Winnipeg. Undaunted, Van Horne began gathering enormous amounts of supplies in Winnipeg. Steel rails came from England and Germany. Rail ties came from the spruce forests east of Winnipeg. Stone was shipped from Stonewall, and lumber from Minnesota.

The work began even while the ground was still covered with snow. It had been a relatively mild winter, and the weather looked promising. Nevertheless heavy rains and flooding waters soon wrecked Van Horne's hopes. By the end of June only 125 miles of track had been laid. Floods on the Red River held up the workers for several days. Van Horne raged. As soon as the waters receded, he called his crews together and told them to lay track even faster, to make up for the delay. When contractors and engineers objected, the general manager informed them, "If you can't do it, I'll cancel all your contracts." There was no further argument. Ten thousand men and seventeen hundred teams of horses were employed laying an average of two miles of track a day. The work picked up in July and August as the navvies moved out onto the flat prairies. On August 19th, a record 4 miles of track was laid. Work crews were highly organized, almost like an assembly line. First the locating parties. Then the ploughs and scrapers. Next, after the roadbed was laid, came the boarding and construction cars loaded with materials for the battalions of track layers. As each gang finished its work on one lap, the cars were moved ahead to the next. After the road builders came the suppliers — trains bringing up building materials, food and clothing, cooks, doctors, carpenters, blacksmiths, tailors, saddlers, and all the hangers-on. Regular train service followed shortly behind the work crews. By the middle of

August, trains were carrying passengers into Saskatchewan. The traffic of incoming settlers continued unabated, even through business slumps in the cities, causing one railway official to comment, "It is a wonder where the people go to."

Van Horne himself was everywhere at once. On horseback, by stagecoach, train, or even steamboat, he moved from one end of the work crew to the other, supervising, chastising, encouraging, hiring, firing, answering questions and making decisions. The work pace was frantic and Van Horne loved every minute of it. "He looks harmless, but so does a buzz saw," noted the Winnipeg *Sun* of the CPR General Manager. His work ethic was simple. "If you want something done, name the day when it must be finished," he said. "If I order a thing done in a specified time and the man to whom I give that order says it is impossible to carry out, then he must go."

As the work crews forged ahead, the smooth prairie terrain gave way to hills. Dump carts and wheelbarrows were needed to replace the horse-drawn scrapers. Water

The men who built the railway often lived in boarding cars like this one. What might be the advantages of such accommodation? The disadvantages?

was scarce, and supplies for the camps had to be hauled over long distances. There were often delays and sometimes the work crews were inactive for several days at a time. Freezing temperatures caused additional problems. It became apparent to Van Horne that the 500 mile goal of main line track would not be met. When the crews finally stopped working in January 1883, the railhead had moved 585 miles west of Winnipeg to what is now Maple Creek,

Laying track on the prairies. Do you think Van Horne realized how much was really involved in meeting his boast to build 500 miles of track in one season?

Saskatchewan. 418 miles of track had been laid over the 10-month period from April to January. An additional 110 miles of supplementary track laid in Manitoba brought the operable CPR track mileage up to a total of 528, not including sidings.

It was a tremendous feat. People who had doubted Van Horne before now referred to his project as "a wonderful accomplishment" and noted that "only Van Horne, with his marvelous energy, determination, and power of organization, and his great faith in his work, could have done it."

The 1882 track-laying year resulted in the use of 57,660 tons of steel rail, 1.5 million crossties, and nearly 3.4 million board feet of timber for bridge structures. In addition, 897 miles of telegraph wire were strung with over 1,600 miles of wire. Right-of-ways were fenced. Stations and warehouses were built and extensive additions were made to the locomotives and the cars they pulled.

MEN WANTED!

A number of Men will be wanted by the undersigned during the grading season this year on west end of CANADIAN PACIFIC RAILWAY. Wages will be

$1.50 PER DAY,
BOARD $4.50 PER WEEK,

During the Summer Months for good, able-bodied, steady men.

Apply on the work at end of track, now near Cypress Hills, about 600 miles west of Winnipeg.

LANGDON, SHEPARD & CO.,
CONTRACTORS.

END OF TRACK,
April 20th 1883

Building Chapter 5
the Railroad

By the beginning of 1883, the CPR had operable track running trains from Port Arthur in Ontario to eastern Alberta. Consolidation of the CPR with other smaller railroads in 1883-1884, resulted in additional lines running from Montreal to Toronto, Ottawa to Montreal, Toronto to St. Thomas, and Ottawa to North Bay. There were other track sections, some built by the CPR and others purchased from smaller railroads, connecting Winnipeg with the U.S. border, and Ottawa with Brockville.

Van Horne's railroad was beginning to take shape, although many of the harder problems were yet to be tackled. The 1883 season found the workers pressing ahead on the prairies, while Van Horne turned his attention to the track yet to be laid around the northern shore of Lake Superior.

Originally, when the members of the "Syndicate" had planned the railway route around Lake Superior, they felt that it might be easier to link up with an existing railroad — The St. Paul, Minneapolis and Manitoba. This line, which took a southern route around the Great Lakes, was an American operation owned by James Jerome Hill, who pressed for the link for economic reasons.

The CPR planned to lay track as far as Sault Ste. Marie, link up with Hill's line which would carry passengers through the northern United States, and then head north to rejoin the CPR track at Winnipeg.

Van Horne objected to the route. "Using Mr. Hill's line plainly puts the CPR at his tender mercies." These sentiments were echoed, somewhat more modestly, by the Macdonald government which wanted the railroad to remain on Canadian soil. The CPR directors were persuaded to change their minds in 1882, and on May 3, 1883, Hill resigned his directorship saying, "I'll get Van

The St. Paul, Minneapolis and Manitoba Railway was an extremely profitable line. How do you think the coming of the CPR affected rival railroads?

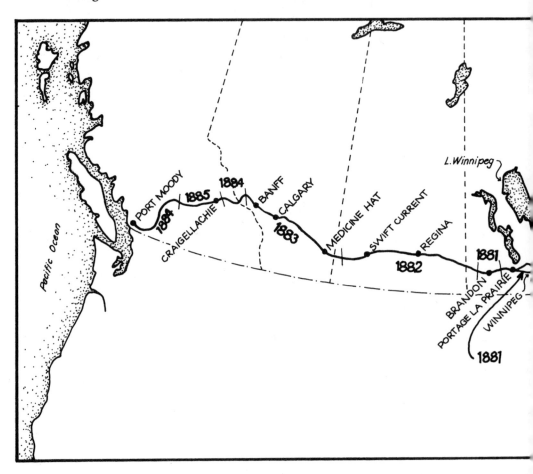

Horne if I have to go to hell for it and shovel coal."
"Well if he does, I'll tear the guts out of his road!" was
the reply.

Van Horne and the CPR now faced one of the most
difficult and costly construction jobs possible. Van Horne
himself defined the task as "two hundred miles of engi-
neering impossibility," and added, "but we'll bridge it."
Building along the northern shore of Lake Superior was
hampered by heavy rock work, the necessity for constant
grading of the roadbed, lack of earth for the construction
of embankments, misuse of liquor, lack of men, and sink-
holes — patches of ground that would suddenly sink
without apparent cause (one such section fell seven times,
swallowing three locomotives and miles of finished track).
Men working on this "muskeg" section had to contend

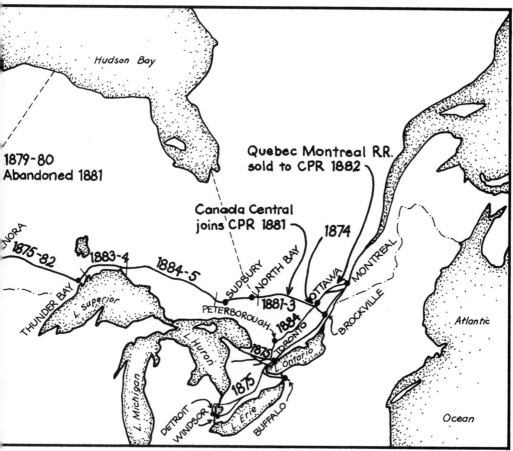

with instable shore lines, tunneling, and ferocious lake storms. The progress was slow. By the end of the year some 160 miles of track had been laid from Algoma Mills east to Sturgeon Falls. This gave the CPR a direct line from Montreal around Lake Nipissing and north to Algoma Mills.

Supplies reached the workers through small lake steamers. Van Horne further strengthened the flow of materials by leasing an existing railway, the Toronto, Grey and Bruce, to carry goods from Toronto to Owen Sound. There they were transferred to the steamers. Inland, the route was blasted out with dynamite which cleared the dense woods, rock, and brush. Van Horne established three dynamite factories in the area north of Superior to save time and money.

The CPR construction proceeded continuously along every segment of the transcontinental route. This map shows dates of completion for individual sections of track. Also included are auxiliary lines purchased by the CPR to supplement the main track, and dates for the merging of these lines with the CPR.

Construction along the North Shore of Lake Superior was hampered by granite bedrock.

Even as the building of the railway was under way, Van Horne sought to supplement CPR service by chartering steamships.

Not all the construction problems occurred in the East, however. Western routes proved equally demanding.

Originally the CPR planned to cross the Rockies by way of Yellowhead Pass, on the northwesterly course selected by Sir Sandford Fleming. In 1881, however, the directors of the company decided that a more southerly route through the Rockies would be preferable, to shorten the length of the line and discourage the construction of a rival southern Canadian railroad at a later date. The new route would cross the Continental Divide through Kicking Horse Pass rather than Yellowhead Pass. This decision presented the CPR directors with a problem. No passage was known to exist through the Selkirk mountain range, just west of the Rocky Mountains. Major Rogers, an experienced American engineer who had been hired by Hill, set to work to find such a pass in 1881. He and the CPR were working against professional opinion which favoured the Yellowhead Pass route. Van Horne favoured the Kicking Horse-Selkirks route,

Major A. B. Rogers

and raised his own objection to the Fleming surveys: "Those surveys will no doubt prove of great value to future alpinists. But I'm building a railroad." Fortunately Major Rogers finally found a difficult but passable route through the Selkirks in July 1882, through the pass later named after himself.

Work on the prairie sections progressed throughout 1883 and 1884, carrying the track to the foothills of the Rocky Mountains.

The workers had encountered little difficulty and a record six and one-half miles of track were laid in one day as the rails approached Calgary. The navvies were not completely isolated, moreover, for old-timers, missionaries, and Indians would stop by to watch the "great serpent of steel" stretching across the plains. Trained observers, like Father Lacombe, a French-Canadian missionary to the Blackfoot, were saddened as well as amazed at the new iron road, for the coming of the railroad to the plains meant the beginning of the end of the Blackfoot lifestyle and that of the other Indian tribes.

The coming of the railroad meant the beginning of the end for the nomadic buffalo herds. How would the destruction of buffalo herds affect the Indians of the plains?

Track-laying machine

One evening, as Van Horne was looking out over the area, he saw a proud, dignified Indian chief come to the top of a bluff not far away. The chief eased himself from his pony, sat down in silence, and contemplated the new road being built over the ancient hunting-grounds of his forefathers. He left as quickly as he had come.

Nevertheless the Indians were to be heard from soon enough.

The railroaders had been told that the Indian tribes of the 1880's were not as militant as some of their fore-fathers had been. Consequently, workers entered the Blackfoot reservation unconcerned over the rumour of an Indian uprising. The Indians were determined to dis-courage any trespassers on their territory. Under the leadership of their great chief, Crowfoot, the Blackfoot had already held a war council and the young braves were urging their elders to fight if the invasion of their territory continued. The Blackfoot had a genuine griev-ance. The Conservative government of Macdonald had voided any title to any Indian lands required for the build-ing of the railroad but it had failed to warn the tribes of its action and its intention to award compensation for the land taken. Crowfoot, who had always treated non-Indians fairly and expected the same treatment in return, felt insulted and enraged. He had controlled the more militant of his tribe but words of war were now spoken freely. When Father Lacombe heard of the trouble, he

Father Lacombe

rode immediately to talk to his friend Crowfoot. Realizing the matter was serious, Lacombe obtained a large supply of tea and tobacco from the trading post and urged Crowfoot to call a council meeting. Lacombe was able to convince the Blackfoot to allow the railroad to run through part of their lands and the threat of war ended so quickly and effectively that most people were unaware of the real danger.

Van Horne, appreciative of what Crowfoot had done, eventually rewarded the chief, in 1886, with a lifetime pass over the Canadian Pacific Railway. Crowfoot was so proud of his honour that he wore the framed pass, suspended by a chain around his neck, for the remainder of his life.

Crowfoot, Chief of the Blackfoot

On August 20, 1883, the whistle of a construction engine shattered the silence of the prairies. It announced the completed rail line from Winnipeg to Calgary, an event considered so important by CPR officials that the first train on the newly completed line carried not only Van Horne but also a distinguished group of his friends and builders of the road including George Stephen and Donald Smith (later Lord Strathcona). Father Lacombe joined the group at Calgary.

The year 1884 saw the completion of the section between the summit of the Rockies and the foot of the Selkirks at Beavermouth. 169 miles of track were laid for this section in the two seasons of 1884-1885. The net decrease in track altitude over this relatively short dis-

Opposite: The Surprise Creek trestle was 180 feet high. Note the man standing on the right side of this bridge.

tance was a staggering 4,100 feet. Roadbeds had to be blasted from sheer rock walls, towering trestles had to be built over river canyons and supported against possible winter damage. The Mountain Creek Bridge alone, on the eastern slope of the Selkirk mountains, was 164 feet high, 1,086 feet long, and contained over 2 million board feet of lumber. Sometimes even the railroaders themselves quailed before these heights. When one engineer refused to take his locomotive over such a trestle, Van Horne comandeered the cab. "If you ain't afraid of getting killed, with all your money," said the embarrassed engineer, "I ain't afraid either."

"We'll have a double funeral — at my expense, of course," retorted Van Horne, and the engine passed over the trestle without incident.

Building on this British Columbia section of the railway had begun in May 1880 under the charge of Andrew Onderdonk, a private New York contractor hired by the Syndicate. The first complete line, 136 miles from Port Moody to Cisco, however, was finished four years later in 1884. Laying track through the mountains was a particularly difficult and dangerous task for the railway builders because engineers and crews had to contend with solid rock, deep gorges, narrow winding ledges (on which even the pack-ponies occasionally lost

Mountain Creek trestle under construction

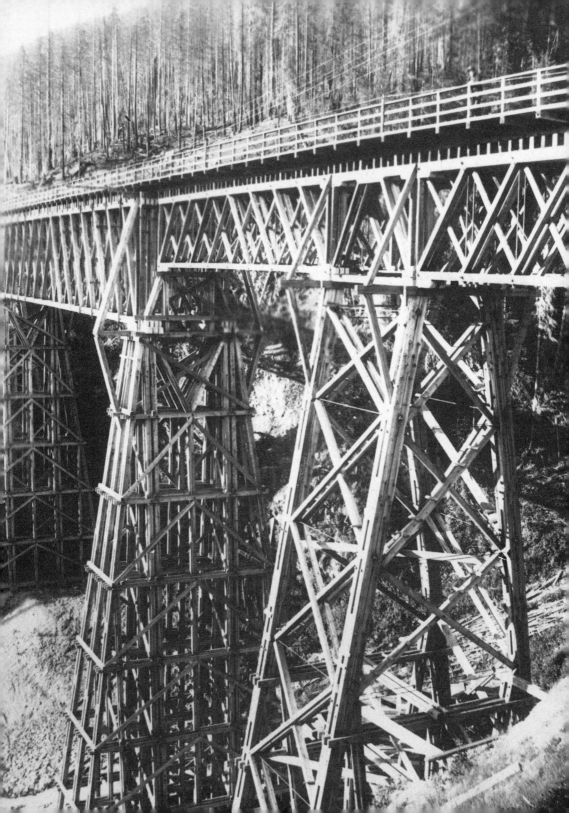

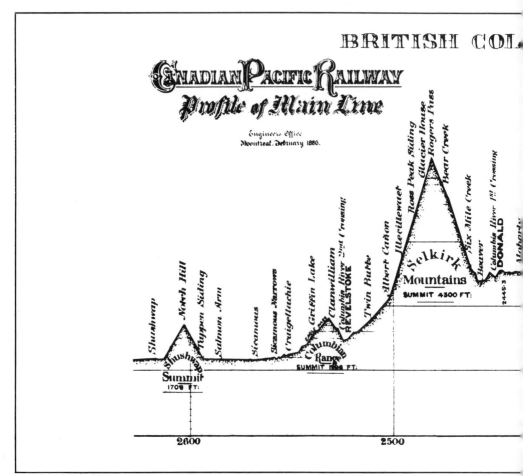

BRITISH COL.

CANADIAN PACIFIC RAILWAY
Profile of Main Line

Engineers Office
Montreal. February 1886.

Shushwap

North Hill

Tappen Siding

Salmon Arm

Sicamous

Sicamous Narrows

Craigellachie

Griffin Lake

Clanwilliam

Columbia River 2nd Crossing

REVELSTOKE

Twin Butte

Albert Cañon

Illecillewaet

Ross Peak Siding

Glacier House

Rogers Pass

Bear Creek

Six Mile Creek

Columbia River 1st Crossing

Beaver

DONALD

Selkirk Mountains
SUMMIT 4300 FT:

Columbia Range
SUMMIT 1888 FT.

2445·3

Shushwap Summit
1709 FT:

2600   2500

*Construction through the
Selkirks and the Rocky
Mountains proceeded at
altitudes of up to a mile
high.*

their footing and fell to their death in the gorges below),
torrential streams, rapids, labour strikes, snowfalls —
with avalanches, tunnels and rough forest areas. Sir
Sandford Fleming, who was not only an engineer but also
a highly experienced explorer, wrote later that he had
never encountered anything like it before and gave the
nickname of *"mauvais pas"* ("terrible pass") to Kicking
Horse Pass.

As the construction of the CPR progressed, Van
Horne was faced with shortages of money. Building costs
had soared and profits were still in the future. In addition,
European financiers were extremely leery of railroad
ventures because of early failures.

Van Horne was confident of the company's success,

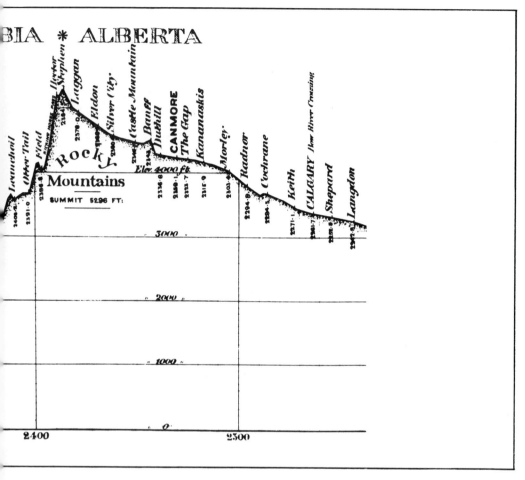

and boldly announced to his own creditors that they should, "Go sell your boots and buy CPR stock!" Finally, however, both he and Stephen were forced to turn to the politicians in order to gain additional financial support. They chose two of the most astute and determined political men of the day — Sir John A. Macdonald and Sir Charles Tupper to work on the opposition lobby. This was a task of no little difficulty for Liberal feeling against the CPR was high. Opposition leaders declared that the railroad would be "an idle, ice-bound, snow-covered route for six months of the year," and that the mountain section "would not pay for the grease on the axles." Ultimately, however, the Conservatives succeeded in passing a bill authorizing a loan of $22,500,000 to the CPR with the understanding that the construction would be finished two years later in 1886. Smith pacified the stockholders, and Van Horne boldly attacked the competition — the Grand Trunk Railway. (He offered to buy the section of their line from Montreal to Quebec and give it to a CPR subsidiary, but his offer was refused.) Temporarily freed from financial worry, the CPR management could turn again to the construction of its transcontinental track. Van Horne was made a vice-president of the company in May, 1884, and Donald Smith joined the executive committee. The railroaders were ready for the last big drive.

Problems Chapter 6
and Triumph

In 1885, Van Horne faced problems both in the Lake
Superior construction and the British Columbia contracts.
Final work on the connective line between Sudbury and
Port Arthur, Ontario, was yet to be completed, and
western crews in British Columbia were laying track at
both ends of the distance between Port Moody and the
Selkirk mountains.

Work on the Lake Superior section moved ahead in
spurts as the builders had to contend with shifting and
unstable river banks. The presence of sink-holes caused
additional problems, and Van Horne was forced to order
trestles built across some of the more diffcult land areas.

Again the CPR faced a cash shortage. Although the
1884 government loan had seemed ample at the time,
its resources were soon spent in the railroad's constant
battles against uneven terrain and weather. George
Stephen approached John A. Macdonald again for more
funds, but was rebuffed. Long, lonely vigils in the ante-
chambers of the various political dignitaries followed,
but to no avail. The Canadian Government would not
step in to help the CPR. Macdonald, although personally
in favour of the railroad, could not risk his political
career by granting another loan. Wild rumours circu-
lated: the CPR was merely a scheme for a few people to
achieve personal riches; the company could not meet a
dividend payment; the company's stock was being
attacked in the London market. Construction crews
often went for several weeks at a time without pay, and
the western crews in particular were plagued by strikes.
James Ross, manager for the western section, sent Van
Horne this report on his men:

After I received the first notice of a general strike, they telegraphed
me they had checked the men interfering with those willing to
work.

CPR construction camp in the mountains.

Kicking Horse Pass construction, 1885

Afterwards I received another that the rioters had gained a victory and were marching in force. I immediately got out and met them at End Track; at the first, fired by their zeal, they had closed all saloons, and were protecting all property, but during the night, the whiskey men succeeded in supplying the ringleaders with liquor, and on Saturday we had a riot.

The Police could do nothing, and matters looked very serious, the men being well armed and firing indiscriminately.

I went amongst them and said that I would guarantee them nothing as to their pay until I knew that I had the money; that I would feed them at End of Track that day, but if they did not leave by night, I would charge every man fifty cents a meal and not pay a dollar until every man was in his camp, and also hold them as a body.

I led them to understand we were prepared for a fight on these points. In the meantime, I asked Captain Steele, who was unfortunately ill in bed, to gather all his men at end track, to be prepared for a fight and to swear all our men in as specials. On Sunday and Monday, I borrowed every dollar I could get, giving my personal cheque when nothing else would answer; I have reserved some money expecting trouble.

February passed into March. The CPR machine was slowly grinding to a halt for lack of funds. Van Horne instructed his purchasing agent to stall the creditors and to avoid paying cash for anything. Still the money was not forthcoming.

Finally on March 26, 1885, Van Horne received the following telegram from his Eastern Manager, Harry Abbott.

MINISTER OF MILITIA REQUIRES
TO SEND 400 MEN THROUGH TO
WINNIPEG AND I AM ARRANGING
TO SEND THEM TO EAST END ROSS'
TRACK AND HAVE ASKED ROSS TO
PROVIDE TEAMS AND PROVISIONS
TO TAKE THEM THROUGH. PRE-
SUME I AM RIGHT IN DOING ALL
I CAN TO FORWARD MATTERS.

H. ABBOTT

The second North West Rebellion under the leadership of Louis Riel had begun. Government troops were needed urgently in the Northwest, and the CPR was the only means of moving them there quickly. Van Horne was ready. The first contingent of troops reached the end of the eastern track section northwest of Sudbury on March 29, 1885. A rapid overland trek — which was stopped twice daily for chicken dinners at CPR expense — was

Canadian troops assembling at the Winnipeg Station just after their arrival from Montreal and Toronto. They are on their way to put down the second North-West Rebellion — 1885.

required before the troops could climb back into the railroad cars at Red Rock (the western end of track) for the 24-hour ride to Winnipeg. They arrived hale and hearty, singing "The Girl I Left Behind Me" as they marched into the Winnipeg station. Total travelling time between Montreal and Winnipeg was seven days — as opposed to three months during the first Riel rebellion. It was an impressive showing for the company.

The CPR transported a total of 2,750 Canadian troops and officers during the first two and one-half weeks of the rebellion, and the outbreak was put down. Despite the disastrous construction costs of running fully laden trains over half-finished track, the CPR had established itself as an important means of binding the Canadian continent. Surely the government would recognize the railroad's worth and grant it the funds necessary to complete construction.

March passed into April and still Macdonald refused to support a bill for financial aid as he feared that he could not get it passed through Parliament. The CPR directors lost hope. Stephen, who foresaw not only the bankruptcy of the company but also the loss of his personal fortune, wept. Van Horne dug in his heels, refusing to admit defeat.

I'm not going to the States. I'm not going to leave the work I've begun, and I am going to see it through. I'm here to stay. I can't afford to leave until this work is done, no matter what position is open to me in the United States.

Slowly, however, as the days continued to pass without relief, even the strong-willed Van Horne was forced to admit, "If the government doesn't give in, *we are finished!*"

Finally, on April 30, 1885, political pressures exerted on the Prime Minister worked and Macdonald was made to realize the necessity of continuing with the CPR project. He sponsored another relief bill, but it was not until July 20 that the legislation received royal assent. Needless political stalling almost cost Canada its transcontinental railroad, a lesson the directors of the CPR never forgot. There were to be other times of financial distress for the company but never again would the directors ask the government for financial aid.

On through July, August, September, and October, the railroad crews worked furiously to complete the line. The Superior section was finished in May, 1885, and the last spike driven just west of the Jack Fish Tunnel on May 16. This officially completed the CPR track running from Montreal to Winnipeg. Track ballasting, upgrading, the installations of permanent stations, sidings, and water tanks — plus the reoccurrence of the aggravating sink-hole problem, however, held up regular service along the route. Freight trains began travelling between Montreal and Winnipeg in October. The first passenger trains began their runs on November 2, 1885.

By August 1885, Van Horne was able to fix an approximate date for the completion of his railroad, and he was pressed by newspapermen, politicians, business associates, and well-wishers for details of the final ceremony. Time after time he was forced to clarify his initial position with regard to the driving of the last spike.

There is to be no "golden spike" driven on the completion of the Canadian Pacific and no excursion to celebrate the event. The last spike will probably be driven by one of our track-laying gang and will be an iron one. The report about the proposed Parliamentary excursion originated in some of the newspapers without the knowledge of the Company.

Typical CPR mountain station and telegraph office, c. 1886-9. The picture was taken by Boorne & May, photographers from Calgary, and they have managed to include an advertisement for their firm in this picture. Can you find it?

We hope to lay the last rail in our main line about the middle of next month, but there will be no celebration of any kind, and it is not likely even that any of our Directors will witness the event.

His Excellency the Governor General is just starting for a trip over our line and is going through to British Columbia. He will probably return Eastward about the time the last rail is laid and we may possibly be able to secure his services in driving the last spike, which will not be of silver or gold, but of plain iron. In any event, there will be nothing like a celebration and no excursion. Indeed I do not see how an excursion would be arranged that would not result in a vast deal of disappointment and ill feeling. We considered the matter some time ago, but when we attempted to fix limits for the necessary invitations, we were utterly lost.

By October 8th, track running east from Port Moody had reached Revelstoke. Rain and troubles with grading held up the work slightly, but by October 26th Van Horne was in receipt of the following telegram from James Ross, his construction manager:

Onderdonk and his western crew reached the Eagle Pass rendezvous five weeks before construction crews from the east were able to close the gap.

NOTICE!

YALE, B. C., SEPT. 26, 1885.

AS OUR LAST RAIL FROM THE PACIFIC
HAS BEEN LAID IN
Eagle Pass to-day,

And the balance of work undertaken by the CANADIAN PACIFIC RAIL-WAY COMPANY between Savona and point of junction in Eagle Pass will be Completed for the Season on WEDNESDAY,

ALL EMPLOYEES
WILL BE DISCHARGED

On the Evening of September Thirtieth.

Application for position in the Operation Department for the present may be made to M. J. HANEY, but the above portion of line will not be operated until Notice is given to that effect by the VICE PRESIDENT.

ALL ACCOUNTS

Should be liquidated before the TENTH PROXIMO, at Yale, as the books of the Company should be closed on that day.

A. Onderdonk.

HAVE HAD THREE DAYS RAIN AND
STILL RAINING. EVERYTHING OUT
OF WAY TO FINISH TRACK IF
WEATHER WILL PERMIT. EXPECT
JOIN RAILS THURSDAY OR FRIDAY
NEXT WEEK IF WEATHER NOT TOO
BAD. WILL ADVISE YOU LATER IF
ANY CHANGE.   JAS. ROSS.

The last iron spike of the millions linking Montreal
with the west coast was driven at 9:22 A.M. on November
7, 1885, at Craigellachie, in Eagle Pass, between Sicamous
and Revelstoke. It was a rainy, misty day, and the ceremony was both simple and short, in accordance with
Van Horne's wishes. Major Rogers held the spike for
Donald Smith, who was surrounded by Van Horne,

*Van Horne received hun-
dreds of congratulatory
letters, telegrams, and
tokens following the
Craigellachie ceremony.*

Sandford Fleming, other dignitaries, and company executives, as well as the workingmen, and navvies, without whose hard labour the scene would not have happened. There were no politicians present. By all accounts, Smith, who had probably never used a spike hammer before in his life, actully bent the first spike, and a replacement had to be obtained before the ceremony. Van Horne's speech on the occasion was brief:

Why is the photograph of the driving of the last spike considered "The great Canadian photograph?"

"All I can say is that the work has been well done in
every way."

After the ceremony, Van Horne, Smith, Sandford
Fleming and the other dignitaries climbed back onto their
special train to complete their journey through to Port
Moody. It was a CPR conductor who summed up the
event best, before going on about his duties, calling out,
"All aboard for the Pacific."

Chapter 7 The Transcontinental Line

Although the Craigellachie ceremony marked the official end of track-laying for the new railroad, it was not until seven months later that regular CPR passenger and freight service was inaugurated. Track ballasting, as well as the building of sidings, water tanks, stations and other facilities, still had to be completed on the western track sections before effective operations could begin. In addition sleeping and dining cars had to be purchased and other CPR rolling stock increased. So, it was not until 8 P.M. on June 28, 1896 that the first scheduled through train, #1, The Pacific Express, was able to chug out of the Montreal station on its way to Port Moody. The trip took 139 hours, and the Pacific Express was only one minute late. The experience was summed up briefly by one passenger, a Mr. Salsbury, who wrote:

I must say I had a most pleasant experience throughout the trip across the continent, and every one should take it who can.

With the end of construction, and the beginning of regular CPR service, Van Horne was able to turn his attention to the operational problems of the railroad. The CPR needed a steady stream of passenger and freight traffic in order to survive. And Van Horne wanted to develop new sources of revenue for the line as well. He bought and developed many of the existing railways in the east, adding them to the CPR system, and planned branch lines in the west to ready as many major population areas as possible.

Van Horne built a series of grain elevators in Manitoba, so that grain could be stored in bulk quantities for shipping east. (One such elevator at Fort William held a million bushels — and Van Horne's critics scoffed at

CANADIAN PACIFIC RAILWAY COMPANY.

FORM 71.

TELEGRAM

To W C Van Horne   Winnipeg

85-1   July 3   1896

Regular through train
Arrived here sharp
on time big demonstration
address from Mayor
& city council everything
passed off in first class
shape

                    JM Egan

CANADIAN PACIFIC RAILWAY COMPANY.

Form 71.

TELEGRAM

To W C Van Horne   11.39 a   134114   Pt Moody 4th

                    July 6   1886

No 1 arrived Port Moody sharp on time.
about 150 passengers mostly with through tickets

                    H Abbott

CPR train #1, The Pacific Express, left Montreal on June 28, 1896 and arrived in Port Moody 139
hours later, only 1 minute late. Van Horne monitored the train's progress across the country
through reports sent in by his track managers.

him for believing there was that much grain to be found in the west). Under Van Horne, the CPR began to offer farmers 50¢ a bushel for grain, while wheat brokers bid only 35¢. And when one group of farmers protested the high CPR freight rates, Van Horne told them, "Raise less hell and more wheat." Flour mills were begun at Lake-of-the-Woods (these mills would eventually rank among the greatest in the world), and timber land was purchased in Ontario.

Van Horne even initiated a full scale advertising effort on behalf of his line. Colourful posters announced the advantages of rail travel:

PARISIEN POLITENESS
On the Canadian Pacific Railway

"HOW HIGH WE LIVE," Said the Duke to the Prince
On the Canadian Pacific Railway

BY THUNDER!
Bay Passes Canadian Pacific Railway

GRUB GALORE
On the Canadian Pacific Railway

And when the new Montreal station opened, a large sign proclaimed in block type, on a fence on the north side of St. Antoine Street:

"BEATS ALL CREATION,
the New C.P.R. Station!"

In 1886 Van Horne made the first of what was to be a series of annual inspection tours from Montreal to the Pacific. While on this trip, he was able to observe the work in progress as temporary structures, such as bridges, trestles, culverts, and roadbeds, were converted into permanent track fixtures. He noticed the increasing immigrant movement into the prairie sections and saw that grazing land was filling up with prime cattle from Eastern Canada and the United States. In the mountain areas he observed the workers building snowsheds to protect the line against avalanches (always a danger during the winter months). These did not entirely solve the avalanche problem for engineers reported new slides every year, and new snowsheds had to be built accord-

CONSUMMATED!

TO-DAY, AT TWO O'CLOCK P.M.,

First Through Passenger Train

LEAVES FOR

Winnipeg and the West

BY THE

Canadian Pacific Railway.

ingly. (Some time later, Van Horne would devise a system of timber-cribbing on the mountain sides to break the force of avalanches.)

As he continued his inspection tour, Van Horne and his companions passed by new villages, towns, settlements and stations springing up along the route to Vancouver. Van Horne took great delight in naming these outposts after friends, colleagues, builders, engineers, and Indian chiefs. The names themselves testified to Van Horne's appreciation of services rendered to the CPR — Mount Stephen, Mount Sir Donald, Tilley, Crowfoot, Moberly, Cartier, Secretan, Palliser, Keefer, Revelstoke, Agassiz. But there was no Van Horne. Van Horne himself refused to give his name to any of the new settlements or stations. (His wishes were honoured for some time, but years later an alpine climber from Philadelphia named the Van Horne range of mountains in British Columbia).

The first trains halted in Port Moody because the track had not yet been completed to the townsite of Vancouver — actually little more than tents and tree stumps. (The terminus of the line was not actually moved from Port Moody to Vancouver until May, 1887, although Van Horne had long planned to have Vancouver as the last stop of the CPR). Chinese workers were being used to clear the Vancouver area, and docks were being built to the specifications Van Horne had drawn up the previous year. Van Horne also made arrangements for the immediate construction of a hotel. For the finale of his tour, Van Horne watched the first Pacific steamship chartered by the CPR dock at Port Moody.

One of Van Horne's longest dreams had been to see the creation of a complete transportation thoroughfare which would serve as the necessary east-west link for the development of the Canadian nation. The completion of the CPR railway system, and the chartering by CPR of alternative transport methods, established this thoroughfare, and Canadians, in addition to helping themselves, could expect to direct into Canada trade that had so far been enjoyed only by the American ports.

Chapter 8 **President of the CPR**

On August 7, 1888 William Van Horne became president of the CPR, succeeding George Stephen who had decided to retire to England. Stephen's letter of resignation contained a warm tribute to his successor:

> In resigning the position of president of the company, it is to me a matter of the greatest possible satisfaction to be able to say that in my successor, Mr. Van Horne, the company has a man of proved fitness for the office, in the prime of life, possessed of great energy and rare ability, having a long and thoroughly practical railway experience and, above all, an entire devotion to the interests of the company.

Van Horne's election to the CPR presidency was widely approved. As president, Van Horne continued and expanded many of his earlier plans for the railway. He began planning for a full CPR transportation and tourist service by developing hotels in major cities. Looking at the glorious scenery in Banff, Van Horne realized that tourists would not be attracted to the picturesque wilderness unless they had comfortable accommodations. He

Banff Springs Hotel, Banff, Alberta. Built 1886-88. Destroyed 1925.

hired a New York architect to develop plans for a hotel at Banff. The architect proceeded to do so, but changed his mind several times in the process, and revamped his original sketches. This confused the builder, who then built the hotel the wrong side round. The kitchen staff ended up with the most breathtaking view. When Van Horne arrived in Banff and saw the colossal blunder, his reaction was so strong that one observer remarked,

Van Horne was one of the most considerate and even-tempered of men, but when an explosion came it was magnificent.

After his anger died down, however, Van Horne formulated a new solution. He sketched out a rotunda pavilion and ordered it to be built in front of the kitchens. Thus the guests, and not the kitchen staff, would have the desired view.

By the early 1890s, Van Horne envisioned a hotel for Quebec City which would blend in with the city's natural old-world charm. He wrote Stephen of his plans, saying that he would not throw away money on frills but would "depend on broad effects, rather than ornamentation and detail. I am planning to retain the old fortifications and to keep the old guns in place, setting the hotel well back from the face of the hill to afford ample room for a promenade, and I think it will be the most talked-about hotel on this continent." Thus the Chateau Frontenac came into being.

Van Horne was responsible for yet another ingenious scheme. He advertised the first round-the-world tour on the *Empress of India,* which sailed from London via Bombay and Hong Kong to Vancouver. Tourists would return to London by taking the CPR across Canada and then boarding Canadian ships on the Atlantic. This scheme proved a grand success. Van Horne was waiting on the dock at Vancouver when the *Empress of India* steamed into port boasting a full passenger list of tourists, hundreds of Chinese "coolies", and freight cargo. Another CPR employee was particularly enthusiastic:

Don't talk of profits, even if they did run into thousands. The trip itself is worth half a million dollars in advertising to the Canadian Pacific.

By 1893 the CPR was offering tours around the world through its combination of rail and steamship service.

Clifford Sifton

Another dream of Van Horne's, and one he shared
with Sir John A. Macdonald, was to expedite settlement
of the Northwest. He worked vigorously at encouraging
immigration because he viewed the settling of the Canadian Northwest as vital to the fortunes of the CPR.
"I feel sure you will agree with me," he wrote to Stephen,
"that our future is mainly in the Northwest; that we
must neglect nothing in holding and developing it; and
that everything in the East must be secondary to it.
I would rather postpone all of these than neglect anything
in the Northwest." He encouraged pioneer breeders of
livestock to improve the quality of their herds; he even
ordered and distributed one hundred pure-bred Short-
horn bulls and as many pure-bred hogs to responsible
farmers. Van Horne also encouraged agricultural fairs
and exhibitions in Manitoba by granting free rail service.
In order to encourage homesteading, he offered free
transportation on the CPR to hundreds of prospective
settlers who were then expected to influence others.
Eventually the cent-a-mile policy was adopted and it
brought immediate results. (A homesteader travelling
200 miles would pay a train fare of only $2.)

The Montreal Windsor Station opened in 1890. It was
a grand structure with hallways 76 feet long, and front-
ages on Osborne and Windsor streets. The office of the
CPR President was located on the fifth floor. Van Horne
would receive visitors while sitting, legs astride on a
backward chair. As one historian described it, "Mr. Van
Horne's desk stood about where the entrance to the
elevator now is, the elevator and stairway then being
on the west side of the hallway. The general office telephone hung on the wall just outside the Mail Room
counter which was placed across the south end of the
hallway on the first floor. If the president or the vice-
president desired to use the telephone, he journeyed from
the second to the first floor to do so. There were only two
other telephones in the building at the time, one in the
General Freight Office and one in the General Purchasing
Department. Even typewriters were under some suspicion
in those days."

It was from this office that Van Horne conducted his
business, receiving titled personages and railroad workers
with the same lack of pomp. When excited, he would kick

Van Horne at his desk.

over his chair. One memorandum from the Montreal office read:

Any CPR engineer caught racing trains of the Dominion Atlantic to Halifax shall be liable for instant dismissal.

with an addenda to the effect that

Any CPR engineer who allows a Dominion Atlantic train to beat him shall also be liable for instant dismissal.

In 1890 the track extension from London to Windsor and Detroit was completed and ferries were provided to handle trains across the Detroit River. This was followed by the establishment of a traffic relationship with the Wabash Railroad for a connection to Chicago and St. Louis and other western and south-western points.

In 1895, a joint arrangement with the New York Central and Michigan Central Railroads provided for the building of the Toronto, Hamilton and Buffalo Railway, giving the Canadian Pacific the advantage of direct access to United States traffic through the Buffalo gateway.

Van Horne was never an office administrator. He was totally involved with his railroad, and often made inspec-

CPR dining car interior.

Standard design for the colonist sleeping car.

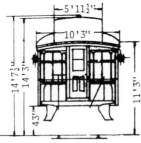

tion trips, tours, and incognito visits to CPR facilities all over the far-flung reaches of the line. Once, in Sudbury, waiting for his train to leave, Van Horne overheard a brakeman bragging about his on-the-job napping. Van Horne said nothing, but upon arriving in his office at Montreal, he sent a telegram to the train's conductor:

> GO INTO THE CABOOSE AND YOU WILL FIND JOHN ROGERS ASLEEP WAKE HIM AND SHOW HIM THIS TELEGRAM   VAN HORNE.

The lesson was not forgotten, and CPR crews kept alert while on the job.

Another time, Van Horne searched in vain for a poker partner on a trip from Montreal to Winnipeg. Finally, he ordered the conductor to play with him. The man obliged. Upon reaching Fort William, however, Van Horne fired the man for breaking company rules — no employee was to play cards while at work. (The conductor was later rehired by Van Horne and moved to the head office).

Van Horne paid close attention to the railway's rolling stock as well. He was personally involved with the increase in height and width of the railway cars to allow for more comfortable seating in the coaches, and larger and wider berths in the sleeping-cars. He added comfort and good looks to the sleeping and parlour-cars by commissioning two artists to revamp the interiors. (Then, of course, he revised their plan to suit his own tastes). And, as a matter of company policy, he insisted that all CPR staff be polite and courteous to every passenger and customer — regardless of how difficult he or she might be.

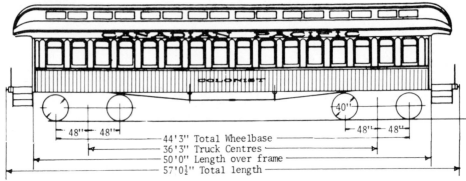

Knighthood and Depression Chapter 9

Van Horne was offered a knighthood in 1890, but he refused the honour:

I would not like such an honour to come to me merely because of my position as president of the Canadian Pacific Railway Company.

Moreover, Van Horne did not want the public to associate such an honour with the upcoming federal election. In 1891 he refused the knighthood again, considering it "inexpedient for the present and (possibly) for several years to come."

In 1894 he was offered knighthood once again. This time he accepted, and was officially appointed an Honourary Knight Commander of the Order of St. Michael and St. George (K.C.M.C.). Although appreciative of the honour, Van Horne also noticed some drawbacks. The old attendant in the entrance hall to his office had greeted him for years with a salute. After Van Horne's knighthood, however, the attendant made a low bow and gave a deeply respectful, "Good morning, Sir William!" This was too much for Van Horne who muttered, "Oh, hell!" as he walked away.

Canadian economic depression had become severe by the winter of 1895. For the first time since 1883 the CPR was forced to cancel the payment of the company dividend. The price of the stock fell to $35 a share and threatened to go lower. Finally a group of German investors poured money into the company. Still, there seemed to be no end to the depression. The lack of development and the restraints on operation bothered Van Horne. He even remarked that the years 1893-1895, "while affording some valuable lessons have given me a chill, and it is quite possible we may make a mistake by over-caution which will be as costly as any that may have been made in the other direction."

By the summer of 1895, Van Horne finally noticed

signs of economic revival. Although the crops were disappointing, large numbers of new mines were opening in British Columbia and the Lake Superior district. In October, Van Horne was able to write to a colleague, "all the clouds in our sky seem to have disappeared."

The CPR had broadened its scope. Originally designed to control the construction of the Canadian Pacific Railway, the CPR under Van Horne had expanded: there were steamships to complement the CPR rail service; there were CPR hotels for tourists; and the company had acquired control of the Manitoba *Free Press*.

Van Horne's major reason for acquiring the newspaper was to offset the often hostile community of Winnipeg. When the tide of Winnipeg public opinion began to turn towards a favourable appreciation of the CPR, the company relinquished its interest in the newspaper's editorial policy. Van Horne was as blunt with the journalists as he was with railroad men. He had certain ideas as to how a newspaper should function in a new country and he made these known in no uncertain terms. He suggested that the Manitoba *Free Press* encourage up-to-date ideas of town planning. "It should speak more as if it had a purpose in this world than as if the reason of its existence had to be justified."

The year 1897 saw the beginnings of prosperity after four years of hardship and depression. Many of the established farmers realized good profits, the discovery of gold in the Yukon contributed to a flow of people, and the traffic of the CPR picked up largely because of the rapid development of mining in British Columbia and the Lake-of-the-Woods area. This increase in CPR business meant the expansion of elevators, terminal facilities, mining spurs, sidings and additions to the rolling-stock. New lines were acquired and expanded. New steamships purchased. A vigorous immigration policy, under the leadership of Clifford Sifton as head of the Department of the Interior, had begun. Van Horne was delighted, but as one of his friends pointed out,

Did it ever strike you that he has the CPR almost finished now — a great work securely established, a success that no one or nothing can possibly break? And just because it is a finished thing, Van Horne positively is losing interest in it? I believe he will get out as soon as he can.

Later Days Chapter 10

By 1899 Van Horne was planning his retirement. "I have
enough," he wrote to a friend, "for my wants and those
of my family, and just as soon as I can be relieved of my
duties, I owe it to others in the Canadian Pacific Railway
Company to leave."

On June 12, 1899, he resigned the presidency of the
CPR, although he remained on the Board of Directors.

Shortly thereafter he took a holiday in California on
his private rail-car, the "Saskatchewan." (The Saskatchewan was no ordinary rail-car! Constructed of mahogany,
it had an interior lit by brass lamps. The master bedroom
had a brass bedstead fastened to the floor.) But the
holiday was not a success. "I got as far as Monterey,"
Van Horne said later. "I went out on the verandah, sat
down and smoked a big cigar. Then I got up and looked
at the scenery. It was very fine. Then I sat down again
and smoked another cigar. Then I jumped up and tele-
phoned for my car to be coupled to the next train, and by
jinks, I was never so happy in my life, as when I struck
the CPR again."

Retirement was not an easy occupation for Van
Horne. His was not a leisurely nature and he chafed at
the bit. His interests were wide, and he pursued his many
hobbies actively. He was a great reader, often finishing
off a book in a single sitting. His literary tastes were not
intellectual as he once explained to one of his acquain-
tances:

I don't care a rap why people do things in novels or real life.
Working out motives is about as useful as a signboard on Niagara
Falls.

   Give me a book for use. If the margins are too wide, cut them
down. If the covers are too clumsy, tear them off. If you buy a
book as a work of art, throw it in your cabinet and order a modern
edition for reading.

He delighted in playing practical jokes, and his childhood
love of geology was retained throughout his life. Nine
new fossil specimens discovered by Van Horne were
named "van hornei" in his honour.

Van Horne's many properties were another interest.
While on a scouting mission for the CPR in the late 1880s,
he had purchased the greater part of Minister's Island
near St. Andrews, New Brunswick. There he designed
and built a spacious and handsome summer home. He
even attended to the landscaping, providing for vine-
yards, peach orchards, and greenhouses. The estate con-
sisted of about six hundred acres of farming and timber
lands. Van Horne became a gentleman farmer. He erected
large barns, stables and silos, and even imported a herd
of Dutch cattle. He raised trumpet flowers, and mush-
rooms — and became an expert at mushroom identifica-
tion. Van Horne named his summer home "Covenhoven"

*Van Horne's Montreal
studio.*

Covenhoven

and enjoyed its seclusion as a means "to get away from the world." Covenhoven exemplified its owner's love of bigness, with its large roofs, doors, windows and open spaces. The living room was so huge it took eight men to lift the Indian rug bought to cover the floor. And the fireplace was twenty feet of solid granite with Italian pillars.

Another Van Horne holding was the four-thousand acre wheat and cattle farm near Selkirk, Manitoba. And finally, there was the enormous greystone house in Montreal at 1139 Sherbrooke Street. Remodelled and enlarged by Van Horne so that it became a three-storey, 52-room mansion, the Montreal house was built like an armoury. This home was the showcase for Van Horne's vast collections of paintings, ceramics, Japanese pottery, bronzes, tapestries and antique ship models.

William Van Horne was a gourmand and, after being knighted in 1894, he announced that his coat-of-arms would be, "a dinner horn pendent upon a kitchen door." He loved food, and lots of it. One of his life philosophies was summed up with the words, "Oh, I eat all I can; I drink all I can; I smoke all I can; and I don't give a damn about anything!" His poker games were supplemented by snacks of caviar, whiskey, and pungent cigars.

Van Horne's major interest, aside from railroading, was art and art collection. His tastes varied, and his purchases always reflected his personal appreciation of the work, for he did not believe in buying only for investment. "The purchase of a picture is like the selection of a wife," he once said. "Never buy one that you don't fall in love with." His 200 paintings — including works by Turner, Hogarth, El Greco, Renoir, Rubens, Titian, Murrillo, Rembrandt, Goya, da Vinci, Franz Halls and Velasquez — were valued at over three million dollars. (After his death, the collection was partially broken up and sold. Many pieces were given to the Montreal Museum of Fine Arts.)

Van Horne was himself a painter — of primitive technique, but this was more than compensated for by his enthusiasm. One of his favourite pranks was to escort some visitor through his picture gallery — stopping every few minutes to mention some tidbit about each master's painting. Finally, Van Horne would stand in front of a

Moonlight on the St. Croix River, Sir William Van Horne, artist.

particularly primitive landscape and breathe an audible sigh of appreciation. The unsuspecting guest would move up for a closer look at this fine piece — why otherwise should Van Horne sigh so? Suitaby impressed, the visitor would summon up whatever words of praise he or she could muster. Van Horne would then roar with laughter and proudly announce that he himself was the artist.

By 1900, Van Horne was back into railroading as the president of the Cuba Company Railroad. He established the head office of the Cuba Company in New York and sent engineers to Cuba to make a preliminary survey. When the report came back that a rail line could be built along the route proposed, Van Horne immediately set about insuring that relationships with the Cubans remained amicable. Amicability was vital since the Cuba Company was working without a charter. Any confrontation would have meant disaster. Van Horne instructed his engineers to build their line south of the Cuba Central Railway.

The Cuba Company railroad was built through a region previously considered impassible and was built without subsidy or any public aid whatsoever. The railroad became a monument to the Cubans' sense of honour and fair play as it was built without "buying" anyone or anyone's influence. As one observer noted:

The Cuban Railway was the purest big enterprise I've ever heard about in North or South America. Sir William relied upon the fact that he was supplying a desirable public utility. He merged the company's interests with the community's, and went ahead, buying no man. It was a fine and most rare side of a business of this sort, as creditable to the Cuban people as it was to Sir William.

The operation of the Cuba Company required trips to Cuba several times a year, and at 60 years of age Van Horne could not be expected to be as vigorous in that enterprise as he had been in the building of the CPR. Nevertheless, he found himself in one of the busiest and most difficult periods in his life. "I have never been so busy as I have been since I quit business," he once remarked. Because Van Horne could not put forth as intensive and personal an effort as before, he diversified his interests. He accepted directorships in insurance and trust companies in New York and Montreal, as well as in a number of new companies engaged in building railways and power plants in Mexico, Brazil, Guatemala, and elsewhere. Simultaneously he was still Chairman of the Board of the Canadian Pacific Company, and was still identified in the public mind with that railway.

During the 1903 depression, the Cuba Company found itself in financial difficulty, but Van Horne was able to secure additional backing in order to continue with his plans for the railroad's expansion. He introduced a publicity campaign extolling the beauties and advantages of the Cuban island. He employed Cubans wherever possible, and initiated a training program which would ultimately result in the Cuba Company's being run entirely by Cuban nationals.

Van Horne was also involved in the development of streetcar systems in Toronto, Winnipeg, and St. John. He founded the Windsor Salt Company, was president of the Laurentide Pulp Company, and was a principal stockholder in the Dominion Iron and Steel Company in Nova Scotia.

Not all of his financial ventures were successful, however. Van Horne lost his considerable investment in a

British Columbia gold mining outfit called the Horsefly and Cariboo Hydraulic Mining Company. Another $20,000 was lost in a futile attempt to develop a local fish cannery near his Covenhoven home. His invention of a magnetic detection device for spotting enemy submarines was summarily rejected by the British Admiralty at the outset of World War I. By 1950, however, the invention was adopted, modified, and improved by the American and Canadian navies for use in anti-submarine squadrons.

Nor was Van Horne's personal life entirely easy. His first-born son died at the age of five. His mother followed not long after in 1885, and Van Horne turned to his sister Mary for comfort and advice. In 1904, Mary was stricken by serious illness, and despite careful nursing by Van Horne and all the best doctors he could summon, she died later that year.

Van Horne's only grandchild, William Cornelius Covenhoven Van Horne, was born in 1907, and the grandfather's joy in his new relative knew no bounds. He was equally proud of the new parents, "Bennie" Van Horne, and his wife Edith Molson.

Van Horne's last years passed somewhat peacefully. By 1910 he had resigned most of his outside business interests, and began to devote himself more closely to the pursuit of his many hobbies. Trips to Europe to purchase artwork, visits to and from Covenhoven, painting, and the visits of old friends were his favourite pastimes.

A stomach ailment sent Van Horne to the hospital in 1915 for an operation. While recovering, the old railroader was cautioned by his doctors to smoke no more than three cigars a day. He agreed. The next day a large package arrived for Van Horne. Inside was a special collection of perfecto cigars — each one two feet in length. From then on, Van Horne kept scrupulously to his doctor's orders. He smoked no more than three cigars a day; each cigar, however, was a four-hour smoke.

William Cornelius Van Horne died on September 11, 1915 — three weeks after his abdominal operation. He was man who loved life in the largest sense of the word, and his one wish upon his deathbed was for more of it: "When I think of all I could do, I should like to live 500 years."

Van Horne was buried in Joliet, Illinois

His body was taken by private railway coach — The Saskatchewan — to Joliet, Illinois for burial, although Van Horne had become a Canadian citizen years before. His death was keenly felt around the world. The CPR suspended all operations for a short period of tribute. Cuba declared a national day of mourning, and Cuban President Mario Menocal saluted the great man by noting, "He did more for us in one year than Spain did in four centuries."

The effect of William Van Horne's work in helping to forge the Canadian nation is difficult to overestimate. His was a personality powerful and heroic on a grand scale.

Further Reading

Berton, Pierre. *The Last Spike*. Toronto. McClelland and Stewart. 1971.

Berton, Pierre. *The National Dream*. Toronto. McClelland and Stewart. 1970.

Canadian Pacific Railway: A holiday trip (Montreal to Victoria). Montreal. Railfare. 1971 (1888).

Dorin, Patrick C. *Canadian Pacific Railway*. Hancock House. 1974.

Lavallee, Omer. *Van Horne's Road*. Montreal. Railfare. 1974.

Mayles, Stephen. *Building of the C.P.R. 1871-1885*. Toronto. Collier-Macmillan. 1974.

Newman, Peter C. *Flame of Power*. Toronto. McClelland and Stewart. 1965 (1969).

Vaughan, Walter. *The Life and Work of Sir William Van Horne*. New York. Century Company, 1920.

Credits

The author wishes to express his special thanks to Omer Lavallee and Dennis Peters of the Canadian Pacific Railway Company, and to Ms. Vera M. Martin of Joliet, Illinois for help in preparing this book.

The publishers wish to express their gratitude to the following who have given permission to use copyrighted illustrations in this book:

Brown Ernest, Alberta Government Archives, 18
Canadian Pacific Corporate Archives, 20, 21, 24, 32-3, 40, 41, 44, 45, 46, 49, 50, 52
Canadian Pacific Photographic Services, title page, 15, 16, 25, 28, 31, 42-3, 43, 48, 51, 52, 61
Chicago Historical Society, 5
E. F. Ott Photo, 9
Glenbow Alberta Institute, 19 bottom, 26, 27, 29, 30, 36, 39
Harper's Weekly, 8
Martin, Vera, 1, 60
Public Archives of Canada, 19 top, 24, 38, 50
Toronto Public Library, 2, 4, 6, 10, 11, 14, 56, 58

Editing: Sharon Rinkoff
Design: Jack Steiner
Cover Illustration: Merle Smith

The Canadians

Consulting Editor: Roderick Stewart
Editor-in-Chief: Robert Read

Every effort has been made to credit all sources correctly. The author and publishers will welcome any information that will allow them to correct any errors or omissions.